(Another book financed on my
hopes and paid for with my tears)

Comedy Album

A Capital Record

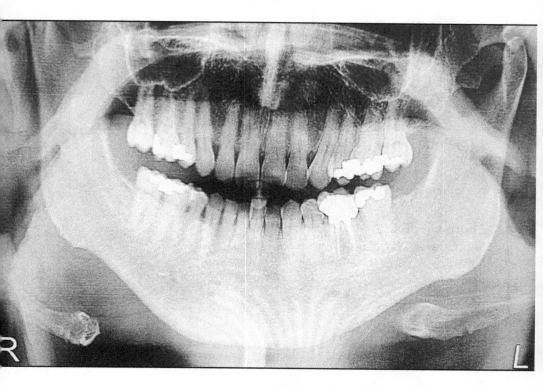

Dan Hendrickson

A Sticky Hat Production
in association with
Lemon Town Limited.

Produced by Flat Sole Studio
St. Paul, MN
www.flatsolestudio.com

Library of Congress Cataloging-in-Publication Data
Library of Congress Control Number: 2020944780
ISBN: 978-1-938237-31-7 (paperback)
ISBN: 978-1-938237-32-4 (ebook)

Photo Credits:
Shutterstock, cover (record)
Tony Smith, cover (Dan onstage)
Dan Ray, 1
Some Guy in the Second Row, 8
Soren Hendrickson, 64
Henry Rifle, 123
Will Hendrickson, 124

Book Layout and Cover Design:
Flat Sole Studio

For booking information, contact Dan at Dan1812@hotmail.com.

Disclaimer: Not everything in this book happened, and you're not going to understand everything that's inside—but I don't either. We're all in this together. That's what I'm trying to say.

To Amy, Will and Soren, as well as my family and friends.

And to Sal Di Leo, J. Marie Fieger and Deb Sweeney

To Dr. J, who is actually very, very cool

To Harlen and Joanne

To MHN and to Becky

Also, to Tricia, Mike and Cheris
. . . and Merwin J. Toomey—and Fiver

That's it.

Oh, and Beck Weathers, David Bowman,
Joe Chip and Linda Paloma

"I don't need a punchline."
—*Kathleen Edwards,* Chameleon/Comedian

Side A

Guy Walks Into a Bar
A bartender walks into a bar.
Behind the bar, there's a flinty duck
wearing a tiny, crusty apron
and standing atop
an old, wooden barstool.
The duck cracks a big grin
when he sees the bartender
and crows triumphantly,
*"You have no idea how long
I've waited for this day!"*

Trout Camp
When I was young,
my parents sent me
to Trout Camp.
But I wasn't like
the other kids.
They were all
trout.

All of us are always somewhere between a rock and a concussion.

Paradise Lost
I was pretty lazy when I
was young.
So lazy, that,
had it been an option,
I probably would have hired
Lewis and Clark
to explore my sexuality.
Who knows what those two
intrepid explorers
might have found?
I guess we'll never know.

Missed Connection
Years ago, I was sitting with an eminently kind
young woman outside her apartment
one clear, summer night.
Nothing happened with her that night or any
other, but it still felt like something might.
Behind us, another couple suddenly appeared,
disturbing our privacy.
So I gallantly suggested that we move
a short distance of about twenty feet
down to the curb.
That way, I added slyly, we would also
'have a much better view of the moon.'
She stared at me blankly, as though
I was speaking cut-rate Portuguese.
To this day, I still think about that night.
And I don't think I'll ever get over it.
That moon bit should have killed.
Killed!

When a swordfish meets a clam, confusion is the name of the game.

One Hoarse Town

Recently, as a joke,
I led a horse into a small-town bar
owned by a good friend of mine.
When we walked in, the bartender said,
"Why the long face?"
I chuckled knowingly at that old saw,
scratched the horse's muzzle
and said,
"It's alright. We know the owner."
The bartender gave me a wry glance
and said,
"I was talking to you, Gloomy Gus."

HE Sells Seashells

She sells seashells
down by the seashore.
She, apparently, doesn't understand
the immutable laws of demand
and supply.
She, quite obviously,
has never sat in
on an Econ class,
not even one time.
Long story short,
she
is wasting her life.

Just because I'm handling your bags,
that doesn't necessarily mean I'm a baggage handler.

Lunar Sea
In a recent dream of mine,
I attended a wedding and then took
a flying cab back to my hotel.
Yes, we're making
remarkable strides
in my dreams.
One night, and one night
soon,
we'll be on the moon.
And from there, by God,
the sky's
the limit!

Lobster Bath
Life often leaves me feeling uneasy.
There are many times where
I feel more than a bit
like a lobster in a bathtub.
I really don't have any idea who
dropped me in here.
Or why.
All I do know is that
either I'm about
to get eaten
or someone
has a serious lobster fetish.
And that's worse.
So much worse . . .

*You have to understand, I'm from the Midwest.
I think all potatoes are sweet. I try not to judge.*

Policy of Truth
I try to write all of my poems
from a position of truth.
And if that's not possible,
I lie my ass off.
Which is fine.
No one seems to mind.

Hash Browns and Gravity
One time I boiled up
a whole bag of spuds,
save for a solitary potato which
somehow
escaped the cooking pot.
That lonely spud sat out
on the cutting board
for a couple of days, and I kept
noticing it and noticing it,
until I finally kind of lost it.
I towered over it, all at once, and hissed,
"Don't think for a minute
that you're safe, okay?
Your nightmare is just getting started,
you starchy son of a bitch!"
To this very day, I honestly don't know
what came over me.

It's funny how, as you age, your attitude towards nudity changes. Starting out in life, you're like, "Oh, God! What if someone sees me naked??" Then by the time you're about 45, it's more like, "If anyone wants to see me naked, there's a showing at 3 p.m. and then an encore presentation at 4:15. You don't have to rush, but I would like to be home by . . . 8:00. That's when my favorite program comes on television."

Aqua City Motel
Like a lobster,
I have a hard-outer shell.
And, like a lobster, I
do <u>not</u> give up my meat easily.
No, if you want it,
you have to work for it.
To pierce my hard-outer shell,
I mean.
What did you think I meant?
Sickos.

Lemon Prawns
One of my very favorite foods,
by far, would have to be
lemon prawns.
To be clear, lemons play
no role in the native constitution
of these prawns,
nor in their culinary preparation.
On the contrary, I simply favor prawns
which are really disappointed
with their life choices.
That zesty angst,
those spiky, bitter notes of regret?
Exquisite.
Just delicious!

I'm not saying I have all the answers.
I'm just saying I hate most of the questions.

Rocking the Cashmere
Not too long ago, I dreamt
I was a crawdad.
It was Father's Day,
and I was wearing a
Cashmere sweater.
Outside of the sweater,
everything else
was normal.
Pretty much
business as usual.

Uncle Sam
When you think about it,
Uncle Sam is the American version
of The Holy Ghost.
I mean, no one ever sees him,
but we all know that he's there,
watching over each and every
one of us whilst we sleep.
And walking back and forth
through walls
simply because
he can.

*In addition to standup comedy and poetry, I also dabble in slam poetry.
Just for instance: "You say that I'm a genius? Man, I'm just trying to
breathe this!" Thank you. You're welcome.*

Inherit the Wind

As I grow older,
I'm noticing my farts
are smelling more and more
like my grandpa's farts
used to smell, way back when.
And that's not good news,
not for anyone.
But my grandpa
would be proud.

Feel the City Breaking

Sometimes people will say things
I truly can't comprehend.
Like when I'm at a party,
mixing a drink for someone,
and they stop me in my tracks
by saying they
'can't do cubed ice; only crushed ice.'
So I dump the ice out, start again
and think,
"My grandpa died in the war for this??"
Alright, my grandpa didn't
die in the war.
However, I'm sure he would have,
if anyone had asked him to.
But no one ever did,
so he decided
to stay alive.

*If I were a Beatle, I'd be The Neurotic One, or The Deluded One.
Or, The One Who Keeps Putting on Weight.*

Or Anything Like That
Do you know what really
pisses me off?
Dungeness Crabs.
"Dungeness Crab."
"I'm a Dungeness Crab!"
Give me a fucking break.
It's not like you went to Harvard.
Or even Penn State.

Lime Rosé
It doesn't happen very often,
but sometimes the universe
spritzes you with love.
And that sounds kind of nasty,
but it's not. Not really.
It's nice.
Kind of refreshing, even.

Mr. Manners
I'm very polite
in bed.
Unfailingly polite.
I always say please.

And thank you!

Whenever someone tells me they went skiing in Big Sky,
I always think, "Size doesn't matter."

Eyes Narrowed
Whenever people tell me that
their eyes
are sensitive to light,
I get upset.
So are mine!
Whenever a light is turned on,
my black circle things get smaller
and whenever a light is turned off,
those same black circle thingies
grow larger.
You're not special, alright?
Let's be clear on that.

Make-Good
I'm sorry that I
screwed your cousin
after that wedding dance
last summer.
That was a true party foul,
and I definitely owe you one.
So next time we go out for coffee,
it's on me, and I insist.
Not including refills.
I'm not made out
of money, capish?

I like to tell people I'm a wolf between the sheets, but I'm a lamb.
Just as gentle as a lamb. Sometimes I get scared!

Gateway Drive
My favorite opening verse to a
poem, short story, teleplay
or novella, hands-down, is,
*"Do you remember that time
you came on the radio?"*
There are so many places to take that.
So many shining avenues
absolutely shimmering
with promise.

Sucker Bet
When I told a friend that
I was writing another book,
he said, *"Oh, is that right?*
More of your vacuum poems, eh?"
"More of my—?" I began,
before letting the question
die peacefully in my throat.
"Yep. More of my vacuum poems."

*Ladies and gentlemen, you may not like fish, but at least they know
how to swim. At least think about taking a few lessons. That's all I'm
saying.*

Tulane Highway (Paul's Boutique)

It really gets under my skin
when I see a man all duded up
in a fine, luxury suit.
Whenever someone like that walks
past me on the street, I sneer,
"Oh, look at Mr. Fancy
and his big, fancy suit!
Look at Mr. Fancy and
his big, fancy shoes!
You know, back where I'm from,
we had a name
for people like you."

"We called you Mr. Fancy!!"

The Farmer (Not the Ladder)

I often think
the world
is stupid.
But then,
I'm a genius.
That's the obvious
conclusion.

I'm having a fight with a friend over a lobster.
Things are reaching a boil

They Call Me Trinity

When you stop to
consider it,
Rotisserie Chicken
is a pretty lofty handle,
for a fairly lowly bird.
If I were a Rotisserie Chicken,
I at least like to think that I
would say,
*"Please.
Call me Chicken."*

Old Pick Up Line

If you want to
hump my brains out,
please do!
I'll be a mindless zombie
for you.
A really happy
mindless zombie too!

*Whenever my actor friend brings up a topic I don't want to talk about,
I say, "Is this a scene? Are you doing some kind of bit?" My actor friend
can't stand that. He has no defense against it.*

Same Old Gripe
I don't know whether
I'm a baritone, alto,
tenor or sax.
I don't even know
my own blood type.
Hell, I don't even know the color
of my own two eyes.
And if you think this is a joke,
I'm not kidding.
This is my life.
No one tells me
a goddamn thing.

Trout
Just once, I'd like to find a trout
swimming about
in our rain barrel outside.
Not because it would make for
a compelling anecdote to share
at a party or gathering.
Though it certainly would.
And not because it wouldn't be fun
to speculate how the fish in question
might have wound up in our rain barrel.
Quite the contrary, it would be
a true pleasure.
No, I'd mainly like to find a trout
in our rain barrel outside
because I know what we'd be
having for dinner that night.

*Ladies and gentlemen, I want you all to like me, and you
have no idea how much that makes me loathe myself. No idea
whatsoever.*

Right Hook
Years ago, I caught a trout.
Afterwards, I went home
and told my roommate
about it.
He asked if I had caught
the trout down at the stream.
"No," I said. *"I caught him
in my bedroom. The bastard
was going through my wallet."*

She Said, She Said
When it comes to me
and my *"comedic stylings,"*
opinions certainly vary.
Some people find my stuff—and me,
I suppose—mildly humorous.
Other people, though,
are far more apt to say,
*"Are you kidding me?
That guy's not funny at all.
In fact, he's a total a-hole!"*
It's one of those sadly,
too-rare situations where
everybody's right.

*My bucket list is pretty concise. All I want to do is eat a Taco Grande
while watching Rio Bravo. That should cover it.*

Kentucky Blue

My eyes are
Kentucky Blue.
Which is to say,
green.
My eyes are green.
I'm pretty sure.

Iron E

I lost my ironic trucker hat recently.
Which was sad.
But what's making me
feel better about it
is the possibility
that it was perhaps a trucker who found it.
Which would be ironic—I think.
To be honest, I'm not real clear
on the whole concept.
Which is ironic
—again, I think.

Ladies and gentlemen, I'm as patient as a rake.
I can bring a dry sponge to tears! You're welcome.

De Low Renta

Once, not so terribly long ago,
a lover of mine told me
that I 'had a beautiful c—k.'
I bowed my head modestly
and said, *"What, this old thing?"*

Record Scratch

I bowed my head modestly.
I bowed my head modestly.
I bowed my head modestly.
I bowed my head mode-

(Record scratch).

That actor friend of mine, he's crashed on my couch once or twice. After lights out, I wait until it's quiet and then I say, "Psst! Are you asleep or are you just acting?" Then I repeat, as necessary.

Mystic Dude
I'm not a mystic dude.
A lot of people wear robes.
They're very comfy.
The tall, pointy hat I so often sport?
It's just what's in style.
And that magic wand I carry around
with me at all times?
It's funny you should ask.
Obviously, it's solely for effect.
And as far as the various spells and incantations
I tend to mutter under my breath . . .
they work only rarely.
It's a fairly low-percentage game.
So I guess you'll just have to take
my word for it.
I'm not a mystic dude.

You're getting very sleepy.

Theoretical Homesick Blues
My eyes, it turns out,
are a largely theoretical blue.
I only know this because
I ran into a theoretical scientist while
out on a walk one day,
and when we made eye contact,
he said, "*Oh my God. Oh my God!!*"
Then he rushed me back to his lab
and introduced me to his
scientific pals,
all of whom were literally
green with envy.

I like to paint pictures with my mind. Sometimes my brush goes dry.

Same Guy, Different Horse
Recently, as a joke,
I led a horse into a small-town bar
owned by a good friend of mine.
When the bartender saw us, he said,
"Why the long face?"
With a smile, I held up a hand and nodded,
acknowledging that old, classic joke.
"Right," I said. *"That's a good one."*
"I wasn't talking to the horse," he replied.
*"I was talking to you, and what I was
talking about was your stupid,
horse face."*
"Oh," I said. *"Well. That's a horse
of a different feather, isn't it?"*

Hello, Columbus
I can't blame all my problems
on my own sexual ineptitude.
Sometimes I wish that I could.
Life would be a lot easier.
So much easier.
It would be
a whole
new world!

*Whenever my actor friend stops over and says he's hungry,
I say, "How about some scenery?" Get it? Because he's an actor.*

The Synth and the 'Stache

To unwind, I play in a one-man,
seventies throwback band
on the weekends.
The name of my one-man band?
The Synth and the 'Stache.
It's pretty no-frills.
Like the flyers say,
One man. One synthesizer.
One damn
sweet mustache.
Good times.

Crosstown Blues

There was a time not so long ago
when I was driving across town
on the freeway, and my fake mustache
fell off in traffic.
Sadly, I had no choice but to drive
the rest of the way home
with my index finger
curled pathetically
above my upper lip.
Like an amateur.
A goddam amateur!

Ladies and gentlemen, there's a lot of tension in my pants.
A lot of tension. I really need to find a new tailor.

Critical Reception

Whenever I see someone tapping away
on a keyboard in a coffee shop,
I sidle up behind them and say,
"Are you writing a novel?
Is this your debut novel?
In any case, could I read it?
Could I read it right now?"
You honestly wouldn't believe
some of the haughty reactions
I've received for my efforts,
for my keen and genuine interest.
No wonder
no one reads books anymore.
Who needs it?

By The Yard

Don't blame me
if you have a stick
up your ass, alright?
I didn't put it there.
And if I didn't put it there
and if you
didn't put it there . . .
who did?
You might want to kick
that around for a stretch.
Or at least have that stick
dusted—for fingerprints.

My actor pal tells people he's a working actor. Which is ironic, because
he can't get a real job. At least I think it's ironic. But nobody asks me.

With a Slice of Lemon?

I saw my new therapist recently.
While paging through my file, she said,
"So what's the deal with you
and lemons?"
I replied, *"What is this?*
Twenty Questions?
Am I being placed on trial
for my personal views and my deeply-held
religious beliefs?!"

When I finally pretended
to cool off,
I asked her
for a glass
of iced tea.

Gawker Slowdown

Dogs always stare at me
real intently.
And I don't know why
exactly.
It's like they can see
straight into my soul.
I remember one dog who
just gaped at me.
Stared and stared.
And his expression seemed
to say, *"You. I know you.*
I know you well! You used
to be a dog—just like me!"
And me?
I wasn't in any position
to argue.
Not even if I wanted to.

For me, reading is a private experience. Like going to the bathroom.

The Cat Butt Seat

I've been unemployed for a while now,
which is neither here nor there.
But what that's meant is that I've
spent a bunch of time at home.
Recently, we cleaned up our second bedroom
and decided to keep the door closed—to
try and prevent our pets from defiling it.
What's happened, though, is that one of
our cats went ahead and designated that room
his private sleeping quarters.
He's had my assistance as far as that.
At some point in the day, I'll look at him
and he'll look at me.
Then I quietly escort him over to the door,
and let him in, discreetly closing it behind him.
I feel like I'm a cat bouncer.
Like I'm the doorman at the most exclusive
club in the world.
Between you and me, it's something special.
I'm even considering buying one of those
earpiece thingies—to make it more official.

Theodore Worthless

At the mall today,
I saw a woman wearing
a jacket with a cat emblem stitched
upon it.
I'm certainly no fashionista,
but I can tell you it was
a really smart jacket.
A lot smarter
than I am . . .

*Another thing I hate about my doctor? Whenever he's giving me a
hernia exam (i.e. handling my balls), he always whistles The Harlem
Globetrotters theme song. Also not right.*

Wake up! Now Sleep!
We live in a world where
if you're awake,
they tell you that you
need to dream,
and if you're dreaming,
they tell you that you need
to wake up.
As far as describing this place,
that's the best I can do, for better
or for worse.
That's the very height of my powers,
which is roughly the same thing
as jumping off of a curb.

John Cougar
I think I could live out
in the Black Hills.
Things are different up there.
Rugged, isolated.
Remote.
You probably wouldn't understand.
Not unless you were a hermit,
or a friggin'
mountain goat.

I ran into our old neighbor the other day. We didn't have a lot to discuss. We really only talked once when we were neighbors. I said his fence could use some upkeep. What the hell do I know?

Lobster Fence
Once, after a really good night of sleep,
I woke up.
That's happened many times, actually.
But this particular time, at some point later
in the day, I mentioned to a friend
that I had dreamt of a lobster fence
the night before.
She said, "*Like a . . . fence designed
to keep lobsters out?*"
I looked at her incredulously.
"*No! A fence made out of lobsters.*"
Good Lord.
'A fence designed to keep lobsters out.'
Yeah, I'd love to see the blueprints
for a fence like that!
Seriously, where do people even
come up with this crap?

Comedy Writing 101
Did you hear the one about
the tortoise and the
portobello mushroom?
In the end, it was all
one big
misunderstanding.
If a bit pervy,
which it most certainly was.
I don't think anyone
would argue that.

A boat has to be planed before it can set sail.
I find that ironic. Maybe that's just me.

Comedy Writing 201
People say comedy is hard.
It isn't hard—it's super easy!
Take Best Buy.
If I didn't like
Best Buy,
why, I might call it "Worst Buy."
But I like Best Buy!
Some really good friends of mine work
down at their Corporate Office.
I'm just saying, a lot of this stuff
writes itself.
Comedy gold.

North Kabekona (Comedy Writing 301)
I have this friend up north named Paul,
and he has this huge bunion
on his foot.
Sometimes, I swear,
it's too easy.
Sometimes it's like shooting
a bunch of big, stupid fish
in a dumb, slightly oversized
barrel.

My therapist told me to buy a laser printer—to help me get over my fear of laser beams. But it's not working. The damn thing is still in the box. I'm afraid to open it.

Mayonnaise (for Richard Brautigan)
In one of my to-go orders recently,
a restaurant gave me a packet of
"Real" Mayo.
I don't want any "Real" Mayo, thank you.
I want the counterfeit stuff.
The phonier, the better.
Everything else on this world is fake,
so let's keep things consistent.
Don't think for a minute
you're going to come in here
at the eleventh hour,
hand me a packet of "Real" Mayo
and somehow everything is going to be
groovy and delicious.
It's not, and you know it.
Put that on your sandwiches.

Rock and Troll
Do you remember that time
you came on the radio?
It was so exciting!
It was one of your newer songs,
and I remember thinking it was
too bad they didn't play
one of your older ones.
A song that was actually catchy,
and at least somewhat relevant.
But, hey, they played your song
on the radio.
You should be proud!

*I was putting out a radio signal in the 90's, but I was all over the place.
Calypso, jazz, swing, blues—World Music. No wonder nobody was
listening.*

A Kick in the Head

Few things are sadder in life
than getting kicked in the head
by a mule at high tide.
So far, it's only happened to me once,
but I doubt I'll ever forget it.
I was standing on a grassy, seaside
overlook (it wasn't a knoll)
watching surfers below
maneuver through
some truly gnarly swells,
waves heaved up by the rising tide.
At the time,
I was crouched down directly
behind an irritable mule,
and I recall thinking,
"I had better snap to
or I might well
get kicked in the head
by a mule at high tide,
and I would certainly come to regret that
somewhere down the line!"
And I did.
Hell, I still do!
Every time a storm front
rolls through,
my cranium howls
like a mutant kazoo.

I hate it when I run into my doctor at parties,
and he makes me show him my tonsils. That's not right.

Intervention
Few things will change your
worldview
quicker than
getting kicked
in the head
by a mule.
Even at low tide,
it's a life-changing experience.

Stove Top Overstuffing
Abraham Lincoln was
a lot of things.
Among those things that he was,
was a full-blown diva;
a balls-out,
tail-wagging, glory hound.
It's like, 'I'm ten feet tall,
I have a huge, bushy beard
and I'm President of the
United States of America.
But you know what? That's not enough.
Not for me, Abe Lincoln.
No, I need something else.
One more thing . . . I know!
How about a big, tall, stupid hat?'
And we all know how that turned out,
don't we?

Ladies and gentlemen, we live on a world so sick my guitar
cannot heal it. Can you imagine how sick this world must be?

Ask Me a Question

Am I a good person?
I wouldn't even know how
to begin to answer that question.
Who would I compare myself to?
Joan of Arc?
Do not pass go.
They burned her to a crisp!
Alexander the Great?
Never met the gent.
Maybe . . . Abraham Lincoln?
They all but blew
his head off.
Ask me a different question.
I don't like the direction
this is taking.

Follow-Up Question

Do I think people are good?
How in the hell should I know?
If you're really interested in
an answer to that question,
I know a great private investigator.
His rates are pretty reasonable.
He charges sixty bucks an hour.
You can tell him I sent you.
No, scratch that.
I still owe him sixty bucks.
Tell him you don't know me.
Tell him you never
heard my name
so much as once.

*"Judy in disguise, well that's what you are. Lemonade pie . . . and a
cantaloupe saw!"*
          —*Judy in Disguise,* John Fred & His Playboy Band

You Know I Am

I tell you, if I'm not
changing the blade
on my cantaloupe saw,
I'm trying to figure out
what to do with all the
goddamn rinds.
Life!
Am I right?

Indie 500

Poets are kind of like
race car drivers:
We have to know
when to hit the gas,
when to lay off the gas,
and, most importantly,
when to touch
the brakes.
And we also have to know when
it's time to whip shitties
on the infield grass.
Of course, poets don't get
to do that all that often.
If you wanted to be a hot dog,
you should have learned
how to drive real fast
around and around
an oval track.

*I was driving in traffic the other day and this woman in front of me,
driving 75 MPH, was using the skylight in her car as an ashtray,
effectively using the whole world as her ashtray. It was one of those
'Love the sin, love the sinner' kind of things. I was smitten.*

Pack Mule

Recently, as a joke,
I led a horse into a small-town bar
owned by a good friend of mine.
My friend, the owner,
came out from his office in the back.
He smiled when he saw me, and said,
"I thought I smelled horseshit!"
Then his eyes grew wide when he saw
the horse standing behind me.
*"What in God's name
is that horse doing inside my bar?
You can't bring a horse into a bar!
This is a legitimate place of business!!
What the hell's the matter with you?"*
"We were just leaving," I said, quietly,
before loping for the exit.

*I tend to employ a gas station logic. Even when
I'm not making sense, I just keep on pumping.*

Paging Ginger Rogers
There are mornings when
you get out of bed and you
start your day by stepping
in a big pile of dogs**t.
You can't take it personally.
After all,
the world isn't out to get you.
It's out to get me.
I just stepped in dogshit!
As if I didn't have enough
crap in my life?
Now I'm gliding across the floor
on the stuff like I'm freaking
Fred Astaire!
What's the matter with people?
Who thought that any of this was
a good idea?
Or even a half-way
substandard one?!

Keeping the Faith
Whenever I go into a store
or a shop, I always ask if
I'm the millionth customer.
That's my retirement plan.

I hate when you're at the airport, and you drop your suitcase
on your foot. It's like, "Why do I travel??"

Outside the Box

Things happen all the time.
Nothing, and I mean nothing,
can stop them from happening.
Not even Jesus.
Although maybe I shouldn't be
so quick to type those words.
He's already surprised me once.
Turning water into Cabernet . . . (kab-er-net)
now, who else
would have ever
thought of that?

Liars in Love

Sometimes I dance alone.
It doesn't mean that
I don't want to dance with you;
I do.
I just don't want your
weak-ass moves taking away from
the sweet work I'm doing.
I'm sorry if that . . .
I'm sorry.
That was uncalled for.
Totally indiscreet.
You're a terrific dancer.
I mean that.

The ethernet is just like the internet, except even more annoying.

Sacramento Wine

It's a little-known fact,
but Jesus couldn't swim.
He hated water.
It's kind of obvious when
you stop to think about it.
That's why he always walked
on top of the stuff.
That's also why he leapt
at the chance to change it into wine
every chance he got.
Deep down, he wanted to
operate a vineyard someday.
But his old man wouldn't
hear of it.

Literal Bill

People will sometimes say to me,
"What am I going to do with you?"
To which I generally reply,
*"I don't know, but
I feel like I should at least have
some small say in the matter."*
I'm a very literal person.
Figuratively speaking.

When Jesus walked on water, I wonder if it tickled his feet?
I wonder if he did The Running Man—just for laughs?

The Bear of Bad News

I tell people I hate being
the bearer of bad news,
but that's not true.
I love delivering some bad news.
Like,
"Sorry, it looks like
they gave you decaf."
"That new grass you planted?
It's all dead."
Or, *"I forgot to walk your dog today,*
like you asked. My bad."
Delivering bad news like that,
that's my cream cheese.
It's my sweet cocoa butter!

Sweet Dreams Are Made . . .

I had the most amazing dream
the other night.
I was wearing a cinnamon vest.
But there were also definite hints
of saffron and cacao.
My pants were gabardine.

Nobody knows what lobsters are thinking,
until you hear them start to scream.

Sweet-a** Vest
In a dream once, someone
approached me and complimented
me on the sweet-a** vest
I was wearing.
"*That is one sweet-a** vest,*" they ventured.
I puffed out my chest and replied,
"*You bet your ass it is!*"
Then I immediately felt awful.
Even in my dreams, I'm terrible
at taking compliments.

Doc Marten Sheen
Someone told me once that
'some of us are born to shine
and some of us are born
to shine shoes.'
Then he handed me a rag
and said, "*All you need now
is some polish,
a chair
and a stool.*"

*I never see my friends at the airport.
It's like they're afraid to fly or something. I don't get it.*

Sky Lounge

I never see famous people
at the airport. Never!
Not George Clooney,
not Mary Tyler Moore,
not Kevin Bacon.
I'm sick of it.
Do you hear me?
I'm tired.
SO tired.
I honestly don't know
how much longer
I can take it.

What Matters Most

On the way back home
from their month-long Midwest tour,
The Vomit Kings pulled over
and stopped
for ice cream.

Sure, you can put a badger in a hat. But where do you go next? See?
You've painted yourself into a corner. You didn't know when to quit.

Rocky Road
Anyone who thinks the world
is a good place
hasn't lived here.
If one of those people
visited our world,
it would be a day—maybe two
—before they approached me
and said, "*I don't know what
I was thinking. The world is
a terrible, terrible place.*"
And I would smile and say,
"*Welcome
to my world.*"
Then I would take them
out for ice cream,
to show them
that it's not all bad.

*What is it with baked potatoes? Okay, you're baked.
We get it. Now what? These fucking guys.*

Listserv

Every time I see a sign
offering soft serve ice cream,
I immediately pull over.
Then I run inside
and plead with the counterperson
to make my order
'Soft like a dream—so soft
that I scream!'
I have to travel a long way
to get soft serve these days.
I'm on a lot of 'Do not serve' lists.

Gritty Majesty

I'm a big fan of
The Vomit Kings
and have all of their records.
But if you ask me,
their very best album was
Liquid and Chunks.
To me, they just haven't
quite been able to capture that same
gritty magic
on subsequent records.

Life is short, like that one friend of yours.
But I still like her. You shouldn't be so judgmental.

Life of PI

I'm not much of a
private detective,
but I'm always happy
to charge people fifty bucks
an hour if it
makes them feel better.
Plus expenses.

Needle on a Hayseed

You might wonder what gives me
the right to put together
a comedy album.
After all, I'm not a standup.
(gross)
And though I like to play at it,
I'm also not—quite—a poet.
(ew)
What I am is a screenwriting comic
who sometimes writes poems.
I think that's the best
way to say it.

*Ladies and gentlemen, I'm at a point in my life where
tucking in my shirt seems like an awful lot of work.*

Abstract Poetry
Abstract poetry tends to
confuse
the living hell out of me.
Like this left-of-center nugget,
just for instance.

Love me for ten minutes
and we'll lie back
on the sand.
I will be your swordfish
if you will be
my clam.

Yeah, abstract poetry.
I swear to Christ,
I'll never understand it.

Sausage Champ
My favorite mornings
are the ones where
I tumble out of bed,
stumble to the kitchen
and someone says,
"How about some sausage, champ?"
That's almost always the mark
of a good day to come.

As a writer, I'm always torn between having
things to do and not wanting to do them.

Johnny Cakes
Part of me suspects I might really enjoy
being a short-order cook.
The only thing I couldn't do?
Make pancakes for jerks.
I'm sorry, but they
don't deserve 'em.
Fucking jerks.

Bacon-Wrapped Trout
It's tough to wrap
a trout in bacon.
The damn things
won't hold still!

Lobster Trance
It's relatively easy to
put a lobster
in a trance,
but getting them out of that trance,
that can be an all-day project.
Is it worth all the trouble?
I honestly can't tell you.
I guess it depends upon your
schedule.

I've never been to Cape Cod, but I often find myself saying,
"Holy Mackerel!" It's roughly the same thing.

Lobster Vest

You can also put a lobster
in a vest, but people will not
be impressed.
Oh, you might think it's the key
to everything.
That getting that lobster dressed to the nines
will get you invited to the best parties
and standing reservations at
the fanciest restaurants in town,
but it won't.
It will not.
People will just say,
"Why is that lobster wearing a vest??"
You can take my word on that.

Da-Da-Da-Da-Da-Da-Da

In my single days,
I was a lot like The Chicken Dance,
No one really wanted to do me,
but those who did
were often surprised by
how much fun they had.

Ladies and gentlemen, I had a glass of scotch once.
It's one of the worst things that's ever happened to me.

The Leather Pants Express
For the greater part of a lost decade,
I often found myself with plenty of time
for introspection.
Certainly, it was not at all uncommon
to find myself wandering and wondering,
"Why is it always me, me alone,
walking home from the party
at three in the morning
wearing tight, imitation
leather pants?"
It was sometime in the late 90's
before I finally realized, with a gasp,
"It's these f-----g pants!"

Epiphany
Mark my words:
Nothing good
ever happens
while wearing pants.
On your deathbed,
whether you're defiant
at peace or contrite,
you will see
that I was right.

When you're a leader, sometimes you have to take off your vest.
That way, people know you mean business.

Drama Club
My stage name
is Leonine Template.
But I'm not an actor,
so I guess it doesn't
matter.

Both of Them
You don't look
the way I look
without getting plenty
of deep, restorative sleep
on a regular basis.
That's always been a top
priority for me.
I assure you, every single "booty call"
I've ever received has gone straight
to voicemail!

*I'll never forget the time I went camping and almost choked
to death on a compass. The irony alone nearly killed me.*

Message in a Bottle
Back in my younger days,
after a certain time in the evening,
I would switch my answering machine
message from a generic communique
to one focused at a very certain demographic.
Namely, people trying to place late-night
"*booty calls*" to yours truly.
That message went something like this:

Hello. It's very late.
Listen to me carefully.
I know what you want and I
appreciate your interest—I do.
But your desires are not normal—or healthy.
You need to see a doctor as soon as possible.
A real doctor.
One with a PhD!

I only hope my message got through.

MD Beer Bottles
I saw my doctor recently
and he told me I was drinking exactly
the right amount of beer.
Not too much and not too little.
At the end of the exam, he said,
"*When you get home tonight,*
crack a brewski for me, boy-ee!"
My doctor often tries to be cool.
It hardly ever works.

Ladies and gentlemen, if I were a doctor, I'd have my assistant hold my
calls. I'd sit around my office all day eating free suckers.

Much Meow About Nothing
Our cat is conflicted,
just like Shakespeare.
I'm sorry, he's conflicted like
Hamlet.
NOT Shakespeare.
He's nothing at all like
William Shakespeare.
Our cat's a horrible writer.
We tease him about it
all the time!
So repetitious.

Obligatory Monkey Poem
My love is not
a chimpanzee,
so don't put it in a cage.
For that matter, you shouldn't
put chimpanzees in cages, either.
What is it with you and cages?
You know, I don't think
this is going to work out.
What did I ever see in you?!

*I've been a Project Manager, but I wasn't a great Project Manager.
About halfway through a given project, I'd pull my team aside and say,
"Guys, we've knocked down some pins. Let's let Jesus pick up the spare."*

Splish-Splash

Parties are the worst.
They're terrible,
awful things.
Just . . . ew.
But they can be
a lot of fun, too.

Pincher Move

I told my therapist I had a dream
about a huge lobster squeezing two lemons
between its front pincers.
She replied by saying,
"What the hell is wrong with you??
You know what? I don't think I can help you.
I don't think anyone can help you!"
I quickly pulled out my tape recorder and
asked her if she could say that last part
again, so that I could play it back
for my other therapist—in a last-ditch
attempt to prove that it wasn't just me,
that someone else concurred.
Shaking her head in disbelief,
she quietly demurred.

Some people are addicted to gravity. Not me. I can't stand the stuff.

Shackleton
I have long thought about journeying
all the way to Sheboygan, Wisconsin
simply to buy
a toboggan.
Mostly so I could use that ear-catching
tidbit as an icebreaker
at social gatherings
and such.
I am, indeed, quite the
gifted conversationalist.
People come from miles around
for a chance to talk with me.

Specialty Greeting Card
I'm sorry
that I screwed your cousin
after that wedding dance
last summer.
But let's not forget,
it takes two to do
the ol' naked tango,
am I right?
Let's—let's please—not
lose sight of that.
I'm begging you.

*Ladies and gentlemen, I'm a very tender lover. Very tender! So tender,
my partners sometimes forget I'm there. Especially if there's something
good on television.*

Sunday, Sunday, Sunday!
When I was younger,
I didn't have pickup lines.
I had Monster Truck lines.
They crushed everything.
Passion, hope, dreams, desire . . .
there were no survivors.
They crushed everything.
Everything.

Like the Future
One of my 'go-to' Monster Truck lines
went like this:
*"Baby, when I smell you, what I smell
is the future."*
Then I would inevitably stutter
and stammer.
*"Wait. That didn't come out right.
I mean, I guess . . . what I'm really trying
to say, is . . .
I think you smell."*

*Ladies and gentlemen, just because I'm on the lam . . .
that doesn't mean I'm some kind of deviant.*

Still Angry After All These Years
I'm still something of an
angry poet, although I'm certainly
not young.
Not anymore.
It still sometimes surprises me
how angry I used to be.
Like in this poem, which I wrote
back in my late 20's.

Money's Worth
See a penny,
pick it up?
It's not a dime,
you stupid f--k.

So much anger . . .

9.6? 9.8? Higher?
Every time I'm walking
about out in public, I feel like
people behind me are quietly
judging my ass.
Which truly doesn't
bother me.
What bothers me
is that I can't hear
my scores!

Sometimes I wake up and think, "Oh, my God. It happened! It finally happened! I'm in hell!!!" Then I realize I simply woke up with my nose buried deep in my armpit.

Le Camino
I'm ugly up front,
but flashy in back.
I've got a great ass.
There.
I said it.

Obligatory Grocery Store Poem
Whenever I'm bored,
I like to go down to the grocery store
and pretend that I'm Ron Weasley.
I wander the aisles—magic wand in hand
—muttering things like,
"*Accio cottage cheese!*"
"*Accio French Onion Soup!*"
Then whenever I get bored with that,
I take out my walkie-talkie and say,
"*Hermione, Harry, it's Ron.*
Ron Weasley," I add, pointedly.
"*I'm having trouble finding*
the proper cake mix.
We may just have to—bloody hell.
Buy a cake from the bakery!"
With that being said, I slip the walkie-talkie
back into my pocket, walk over to the
cleaning aisle and size up
the brooms for good measure.

Whenever I walk into an important business meeting, I like to take
my pants off and hang them on the back of my chair. So they don't get
wrinkled.

Waffle House

I tend to wish I had a supercomputer.
One that would allow me to run
simulations of me in various situations.
Such as going down to the grocery store
to pick up a box of pancake mix.
Just so I'd be able to observe, evaluate
and weigh the potential outcomes.
All the things that could possibly happen.
If I had a computer like that,
I might never leave the house.
Why would I need to?

Peregrine and Barrett

When it comes to legal matters,
some people say they can't afford
a lawyer.
Others joke that they 'can't even
afford to talk to a lawyer!'
I understand that point of view,
because I myself can't afford
to make eye contact with a lawyer.
The last time it happened,
purely by accident,
she chased me down the street
and made me give her every penny
I had on me—all nine dollars
and fifty-four cents of it.
She sure caught me on the right day.
I usually don't carry around
that kind of money.

*Time is a different thing, a whole separate dimension. I try not to get
tangled up in it. I got enough going on here in space.*

Conversation Starter
Your kitchen linoleum
tastes like rust.
What kind of cleaner
are you using?

Labels
Time is a thief,
space
is a whore,
and gravity?
Don't get me started.

Gravity is a Tyrant
On this world,
if you think you can fly,
you're screwed.
And if you don't think
you can fly,
then you're really screwed.
In either case,
great news!
You've
been cleared
for takeoff.

*A storeroom trance is what you fall into when you're locked in a
storeroom for a long time. Has that been an issue for me in the past?
Let's just say it's happened.*

Dan Hendrickson

Wide Open Spaces
I had a buffalo burger in space recently.
Not in outer space.
I'm not an astronaut (alas).
I just mean the actual act of me eating
that buffalo burger occurred in space,
physical space—in real time.
It didn't happen in a vacuum.
Nothing happens in a vacuum.
Didn't you learn anything
at that school you went to?

Lobsterfest
Have you ever been
poked in the eye
with a crab leg before?
It hurts.
It hurts like a son of a bitch!
I'm telling you,
I haven't been back to Red Lobster
in nearly ten years.

Side B

Loose Threads

All my poems,
everything I've ever written,
they're just a lot of
loose threads.
They don't connect in any
meaningful way.
On the contrary,
they're all clumped together,
like a big ball of yarn.
Sometimes I wish I'd have
taken up knitting instead of
poetry.
At least by now
I'd have
a sweater.

Microscope

I often wish I had a pair
of subatomic glasses.
Just so I could see all the stuff
I can't currently see.
Although it would probably
be tough to find
a case for them.

*Ladies and gentlemen, I know a guy who knows a guy, and that guy
doesn't know anyone. It's sad, really. I don't want to go into it.*

Sputnik
I like to go deep
into Mother Earth.
Now, I know that sounds pervy,
but it's really not.
I'm a spelunker.
I love to spelunk
all over the damn place!
There's nothing like it.
Nothing in the whole
wide world.

Backseat Driver
Do you remember
that time you
came on the radio?
It was awful.
Awful!
Just disgusting . . .

*I don't really say much. What if someone doesn't like something
I say? No thank you. I'm not willing to take that risk.*

Beast Mode
Recently, as a joke,
I led a horse into a small-town bar
owned by a good friend of mine.
I guess the unfamiliar surroundings
caused the horse to panic a bit.
It sank its stupid horse teeth
into my shoulder and clamped down
for all it was worth.
Fortunately, after about eighty seconds
of crazy-intense pain, I blacked out.
When I came to, I heard someone say,
"He's just a dumb animal.
He has no idea what he's doing."
Then I heard someone else inquire,
"What about the horse?"

Baskin Robbins
Life goes on.
People always say that:
Life goes on.
Until you stop breathing,
that is.
Then it doesn't—go on.
Unless it does.
What the hell do I know?
I haven't yet tasted
all the flavors.

I try to count trout at night, to fall asleep. But they're tough to see. The
water quality in my mind has gone straight to hell—which is great for
the trout, but doesn't help me get to sleep. Maybe I should try sheep . . .

Dan Hendrickson

Wet Blanket

You can offer a trout
a warm blanket,
but it's unlikely
they'll take you up on that.
And I'm sure not looking
to rain on your parade.
I love the fact that you care.
I wish there were more
people like you.

Silver Surfers

I hate when you're crossing
a mountain stream and get tripped up
by a passing trout.
I can't tell you how many times
I've propped myself up on an elbow,
with frigid water flowing through
my shoes and clothes,
and shouted,
*"Come back here,
you spotted son of a bitch!
Come back here
and fight like a man!"*

If you want to kick a trout, you have to get your feet wet.

Mountain Stress
To be perfectly honest,
mountain streams
stress me out.
I mean, first there's a mountain,
then there's a stream . . .
When does it ever stop??

Ginning Up Controversy
I prefer meadow streams
to mountain streams.
Mountain streams are trying
too hard.
Meadow streams have nothing
left to prove.

Doubling Down
Meadow streams are quietly bad-ass.
They straight-up
don't give a fuck.
If you want to stand along
their banks and take in
their grandeur,
please do.
And if you don't,
that's okay.
They'll send you
peacefully
along your way.

To catch a vegan trout, you need a tofu lure.

Cutting to the Chase

I remember once, many years ago,
telling a girl I liked
that I wanted to be
'the man who wiped her tears away.'
She blinked once or twice and said,
*"I think I'd rather be with a man
who doesn't make me cry."*
I had to give her that one.
"I don't blame you," I said.
"He sounds awesome."

Candle and a Comet

Neil Armstrong wrote
one good poem his whole life.
Or maybe it was a couplet.
Whatever the case, beyond that,
Neil Armstrong's poetry
was musty.
Thank God he had a day job!
Because otherwise, times would have been
lean, indeed, for old Neil.
You know, had he opted for
"a life of the mind."
I'm not kidding about his other
literary efforts being awful.
You'll have to forgive me, but
every time I look up at the moon,
I seriously want to vomit.

*Neil Armstrong was on the moon. You know he at least thought about
staying! No more traffic, no more waiting in lines. No more over-cooked
Roast Beef. It had to be tempting.*

Brit's Pub

Whenever I order Gin and Tonics,
I always prefer to order them from
British bartenders.
What can I say?
I refuse to let just any punter
handle my limes.
I can do that
on my own time!

Athlete's Feat

I was never very big on
the whole *"I'm great, you're great,
let's go jerk each other off
in the locker room"* thing.
And please don't pretend
that you don't know
what I'm talking about.
If you truly don't know
what I'm talking about,
consider yourself fortunate.
You're probably
the luckiest person I know.
Locker rooms are horrible things.
That's why I always
wear a robe.

Shellfish are selfish, but that doesn't mean they're bad people.

Dan Hendrickson

Follow the Bouncing Balls
I really do wear a bathrobe
in the locker room.
If you want to see my junk,
you'll have to get in line.
And have your credit card ready!
I don't take checks anymore.
I got burned to the tune of
six grand last summer, <u>by</u>
a guy with a checkbook.
I knew there was something
off about that cat.
I can spot a weirdo
half a mile away.
What can I say?
It's a gift.

Pay-Per-View
Getting burned like that,
to the tune of
six thousand dollars . . .
it really soured me.
Can you imagine?
Sixty bad checks,
each one written out for exactly
a hundred bucks.
It makes me miss the days
of character and handshake deals.
The days of customers
you could trust.

I have an MBA. The diploma is hanging on my wall. I don't even remember where I found it, but I'm proud of it. I feel like it was meant to be.

Trust Exercise
I once worked for a business
that was big on ethics.
So I tried to incorporate that into
my poetry readings, via a 'trust exercise.'
At the start of my reading, I removed
my pants and asked the attendees to
pass them to the back of the room.
Then I asked that the house lights be dimmed.
When they came back up, my pants
were long gone.
And I had to do my reading in my undies.
Later, I would learn that each time I turned
a certain way, my wiener would peek out
from its hideout.
I'm probably just lucky
I didn't get arrested.

The Last to Know
I'm fond of telling people
that Del Amitri was my college roommate.
But I didn't have a college roommate.
Not for long, anyway.
No, my unholy screams of terror
in the dead of night,
while I was sleeping,
proved to be what many people
refer to as a "*deal-breaker*,"
I've broken an awful lot of deals
in my time.
Too damn many to count.

Ladies and gentlemen, all I want to do is sing and dance.
Is that so much to ask?

Dear in the Headlights

Do you remember that time
you came on the radio?
You were so ill-prepared.
Your replies were a watery,
unappetizing stew
of poorly-framed answers and
half-assed, off-the-cuff drivel.
I turned the radio off
and, for the whole next week,
made a point of telling everyone
that I didn't know you.

If the Patch Fits

I hate when you're sleeping and
someone sneaks in and puts an
eyepatch on you during the night.
Then, when you wake up
the next morning, everyone's like,
"*Ahoy there, matey!*"
"*Avast, ye scurvy dog!*"
"*Glass o' rum for ye, Cap'n?*"
I suppose I could just peel the
damn patch off,
but I'm the sort of sailor
who believes everything
happens for a reason.

This friend of mine is a skeptic. A real skeptic, too.
He doesn't believe in beef stew!

Sailor's Knot

When I'm really mad at someone,
but coming down off my anger high,
I eventually tell them that
I mostly forgive them.
Which is a lot like securing a
boat to a dock.
It keeps things right where
you want them to be.
If enough time goes by and the
person I am or was mad at
brings the issue up, I say,
"You're still thinking about that?
Man, I moved past that a long time ago,
and you should too. Really."
And, conversely, that same old grudge
can be swung back around
like a spiked mace
should the tides
fail to turn my way.

Tacos with Steve

A few years back, I lost
my prescription glasses.
Which made it hard to see
—or even try to find them.
Finally, I just gave up and went
to a nearby favorite taco shop.
And enjoyed some blurry tacos.

Most of us are like forgotten bottles of Purell.
We could use a few vigorous pumps.

Robotics

Those times I find myself in a heated debate,
I often like to toss out a random fact
designed solely to discombobulate
my opponent.
For instance, I might say,
*"Are you kidding me? If you think that's
what I'm saying, then you can just kiss
my robotic ass!"*
Then I hurry on to my next salient point.
But as I do,
I can almost hear the gears of their brains
crashing to a violent halt.
*"Wait a minute.
Did he just say he has a robot ass?"*
It's so much easier to
knock people down
when they're already off-balance.

*It's tough to be a poet who's also a comedian. And a comedian that
dabbles in poetry. I don't really fit in anywhere. I often feel like Julius
Caesar at a Swordfish Convention.*

Product Spokesperson

Everyone has a snack they once loved
and now consider vile,
truly evil.
For me,
that snack would be
Nutri-Grain bars.
And it's strange, because
once upon a time
I really did love them.
Now they just seem so soft . . .
so perversely squishy . . .
Conversely,
if someone offered me
a Nutri-Grain bar right now,
I would probably say,
"Sure. A Nutri-Grain bar
would be just the thing!"
Welcome to my world.
Good luck
trying to breathe.

Growing up, I never ate my vegetables—which was probably a good
thing. Even without them, I made it to almost six feet tall. If I had
eaten my vegetables . . . I might well have been a giant. Like that cat
in the Bible—the one that David whacked?

Juilliard Shakespeare
I grew up in an age
where people were told winners
ate their Wheaties (a breakfast cereal).
And/or won because
they ate their Wheaties.
But Old Bill Shakespeare
never ate his Wheaties
and look at what all he accomplished!
Of course, if he had eaten his Wheaties
he might well have ruled
the earth.
He could have beaten the cheese
out of Genghis Khan.
Kicked the crap out of Julius Caesar!
Run Alexander the Great
straight through a blender!
The world could have been
his oyster.

True Beauty
I wish you could
see my heart.
It's a juicy, crimson poem.
If you were ever
afforded that view, you'd be sobbing.
I had an EKG once,
and my doctor broke down
when he saw the readout.
He said it was the most beautiful
thing he'd ever seen.
I said, "*Come on, Doc,
you've seen my balls.
Let's keep things in perspective.*"

Hunger Strike

If I could only eat at establishments
where I hooked up with someone
in the bathroom,
I'd go hungry.
Seriously,
I'd die out in the street!

The Fact of the Matter

I'm sorry that I
screwed your cousin
after that wedding dance
last summer.
That was wrong, and I admit it.
But let's get one thing straight.
Your cousin likes to act like this
good girl—and I get that.
I do.
She's real nice.
That being said, at the end of the day,
your cousin
is a bad, bad girl.

*I always know what to think. The only thing
I don't know is why I bother.*

Billy Beane
When someone asks me where I've been,
I get defensive,
closed off.
But if someone asks me where
I've bean, I'll cheerfully
fill in that blank,
telling them everything
I know.
I'm a real sucker for a British accent.
In fact, if someone with such an accent
told me to jump off a bridge, I probably would,
without question.
"Right-o, Guv'nor!" I'd cheerfully chirp.
"I say, Geronimo!"

Astral Turf
Lobsters don't ask much.
All they want to do is
be in foul moods,
clack about in the surf
and pinch shit with
their nasty claws.
And even that's too much to ask!
They still wind up in the pot.
This place, man . . .
this place is tough.

*Ladies and gentlemen, inspiration is fine, but inspiration
never built a home. Oh, wait. It has. I apologize.*

Pardon Me
When you stop to think about it,
the bathroom is a strange place
to hook up with someone.
I mean, I can see the living room,
the dining room, the kitchen, the pantry,
the spare bedroom, the front porch,
the veranda, the entryway, the mud room,
the back patio, the front patio,
the hall closet, the basement, the attic,
the billiard room, the lounge, the conservatory,
the storage room and the laundry room.
But the bathroom?
Well, whatever floats your boat.
If you want to get kinky
on the sink-y,
you go right ahead.
All I want to do
is wash my hands.

Whenever someone tells me, "I get it," I wait around patiently until everyone else has left and then I say, "Do you get it? Really? What's going on here? Be honest with me, what's this all about?"

Lebanon Song

About a year ago, I went out
to see an indie band at a
local, hole in the wall
rock club.
I don't see a lot of live music
anymore, but I liked their sound, a lot.
One of their songs really impressed me
and stayed with me, enough so
that I stuck around after the show
to compliment them on it.
I dropped the name of the tune—Lebanon Song
—and told them how cool I thought it was that
they weren't afraid to get political
in this day and age.
The bassist gave me an uneasy look and said,
"*We're from Pennsylvania, sir.*
Lebanon, Pennsylvania?"
"*Ah, yes,*" I said, while zipping up my coat.
"*Well, carry on.*"

I often tell my actor friend that I wish I knew an actor. Then I quickly add, "No, no, you're terrific. A real professional. I just meant, well, you know: a real actor."

Sophisti-pop
I hate people who fart
in my soup, then say,
"*You haven't touched your soup!*"
No.
I haven't touched my soup.
Because you fucking farted in it!

Short Pants, Montana
When I was a kid,
I once referred to shorts
as 'short pants.'
That fairly innocent reference nearly
brought about complete Armageddon.
My friends Lost. Their. Minds!
They thought, and still think to this day,
it was perhaps the funniest thing ever.
It was kind of like the time I wore
cellophane pants
down to the mall.
Later I discovered that
they also contained
Asbestos.

Ladies and gentlemen, what would you do if you found a moribund clown on your property? Would you
a) Check for a pulse?
b)? Call the police?
c) Call in the National Guard? Or would you
d) Get in your car and drive until you were at least two time zones away?

(Answer on next page)

A Similar Circumstance

Another time where things went completely
off the tracks in similar fashion, I was
having lunch with co-workers and my head
started to itch—right behind my ear.
So I casually unwrapped my silverware
and used my fork
to scratch my noggin,
with vigor!
Not a good thing.
Once again, people lost it.
I didn't see the issue.
After all, it was my fork and
my head.
But they were like,
"What is wrong with you??"
And I was like,
"How much time do you have?"

Self-Improvement

My life has not been a
straight line.
More like decades and decades
of concentric doodles
sketched loosely by someone
suffering terribly from vertigo.
It finally got to the point where
I had to convince myself I was
a comedic genius
simply to keep going.
It took a lot of convincing.
A whole lot.

I'm still not convinced.

The correct answer, of course, is d.

Lime Aid
Lemons are
Country and Western.
Limes
are Rock and Roll.

Arbor Day
I tend to celebrate Arbor Day
by getting blasted on cheap wine.
Then I usually stagger down to the bar
and try to pick a fight
with a random lumberjack.
Arbor Day is always a
real mixed bag for me.
A lot of different emotions.

*I had a dream the other night. I was on a stationary bike in the ditch
next to a freeway. And I was furiously pedaling my ass off as cars were
zooming past me in an endless stream. My subconscious is one ruthless
son of a bitch.*

Lost and Found
The very first time
I toured a lemon grove,
I lost my head.
Looking all around, I exclaimed,
"*Lemons, lemons everywhere,*
but not a one to squeeze!"
Then I clamped my teeth down
on my fist in sheer dismay.
Our tour guide just looked at me
and said, "It's fine, sir. You can
go ahead and squeeze one."
"*Oh, my God. Thank you!!*" I said.
Up until that moment, for me,
it was like drowning.
Like being lost at sea.

I bought a parrot once—for company. But I wound up with this bird that was really private. I'd say, "Polly want a cracker?" And she'd reply, "That's really none of your business."

Matthew Modine
Throughout my life,
I've leaned heavily
on the actor Matthew Modine.
Like whenever I've really loused
things up and it seems all is lost.
What I've done in those situations is
held up my hands benevolently
and lied through my teeth by saying,
"Everyone, it's going to be alright.
I know Matthew Modine."
And that rather unorthodox,
get-out-of-jail-free card always worked.
Worked like magic!
Up until the day I
T-boned Matthew Modine's car
out on the 405 in rush hour traffic.
Talk about karma rearing up and biting
me square on the ass!

Life's a sticky wicket. One day, you're Seattle Slew, the next day
you're Elmer's Glue. This world is tough, man. Tough!

The Horse I Rode in On

Recently, as a joke,
I led a horse into a small-town bar
owned by a good friend of mine.
He stepped out of his office
in the back and shouted,
"Hey, who let that horse's ass
in here?"
Smiling, I looked down at the floor
and nodded my head.
"Yep, that's a good one," I chuckled.
He looked aghast when he noticed me.
"I didn't even see you there.
I was talking about the horse,"
he said, in a hushed tone.
Before adding, in a stage whisper,
"Have you ever thought about
seeing a therapist?"

When I go camping, I don't want to use a Porta-Potty. I want to crap
in the woods—like a bear! Maybe that's just me.

Del Amitri
When I told another one
of my friends that I was
writing another book,
she said, *"More of your
dope philosophy, eh?"*
Thoughtfully, I replied,
*"Well, I'm not sure 'dope' is how
I would—"*
And then it hit me.
"Yup," I muttered.
"More of my dope philosophy."

Mr. Potato-Head (for Sarge)
Life has handed me my head on a
platter on numerous occasions.
And each time it happens,
it only confuses me.
I'm like, *"You know I have no idea
what to do with this goddamn thing.
There are decades' worth
of clear, anecdotal evidence
which establishes this fact unequivocally!"*
But it doesn't matter.
It's like a lifelong game of hot potato
and I'm always the one stuck holding
the molten-hot spud.
What I could really use is a pair
of good oven mitts.
And a couple rolls of tin foil.

Ice cream is nonsense you can eat with a spoon.
Think about it: iced cream. I mean, really

Levi-Strauss Park (Axiom)
If a man
makes up his mind
to wear pants, there's nothing,
nothing whatsoever,
that can stop him.
Unless, of course,
he can't find them.

Tiny Spark Afterglow
Sex with me is like
so many things in life.
After you've had some time
to think about it,
it doesn't seem quite as bad
somehow.
I'm being totally serious here.
You should try it sometime.
It doesn't take long.

Life is like playing chess with small lemon wedges.
The board gets sticky. Pieces wind up on the floor.

Retsyn

I dreamt once that I was
crushing Starbursts late at night
with a steamroller.
When I was finished, I looked up
and the night sky
was black as coal.
I leaned back, popped a breath mint
into my mouth and admired
my handiwork, with a satisfied grin,
and a cold, delicious twinkle
in my eye.

Higher Love

I'm sorry that I
screwed your cousin
after that wedding dance
last summer.
That was probably wrong,
and I accept that.
But on the other hand,
the experience transformed me.
It changed my life—completely.
Prior to that, I wasn't a religious man.
But I don't wonder about heaven,
not anymore.
I've felt it, in my loins.
It's real.

Ladies and gentlemen, if you're wondering about
my nationality, I'm half-Norwegian and half-Peonies.

Listening at Home
Do you remember that time
you came on the radio?
I don't think anyone
was expecting that.
Not even you.
It made for terrific radio,
but as I recall,
the FCC had something to
say about it too.
There are rules in the book about
common decency.
Strict moral standards which must
be upheld.

Overhead
I sometimes wish
I owned a restaurant
shaped like a smokestack.
An actual, free-standing smokestack.
It would be small inside.
Packed in really tight.
There would likely only
be room
for one table.
And it would be awfully
tough to light.

When people tell me I'm not the person that they thought I was, I always say, "Well, who did you think I was?" There seems to be a lot of confusion on this point.

Smokestack

Onstage once,
I ad-libbed that I was
like The Titanic
in bed: "I always go down."
What I meant was that
I go down in defeat;
that I'm the equivalent of
a maritime disaster between
the sheets.
But that line got a huge laugh,
which tells me
there's a better joke buried somewhere
in the wreckage of that first joke.
I just have to figure out what it is.
Then we can all have a laugh together.
Like mature adults.

Meadow Song

I ran into my friend
Jeff Meadowsong
the other day.
Before I could so much
as open my mouth, he said,
"Yes! It's my real name!"
My friend Jeff Meadowsong
needs to chill the f out.
No one's out to get him.

*When we have something that we want to make sure doesn't get folded,
we put that thing in a folder. Life is a very strange thing.*

Jed Copacetic

I also have a friend named
Jed Copacetic.
He's a great guy, but he's
really difficult to describe.
He's like . . . Alex Walking Tall
meets Jeff Edamame.
I told you he was tough
to describe.
Why the hell do people
keep asking me?!

Train Station Blues

Then there was this time I was
standing on the train platform
and a beautiful young woman
approached me.
She said, *"Excuse me, sir,*
but I think your fake mustache
just fell off."
I looked down at the sad, fuzzy arc
resting on my imitation leather shoe
and said,
"That's not mine."
She replied, *"It is. I just watched it*
tumble right off of your upper lip."
And right then, at that moment,
I started to weep.
Tears of real anguish,
tears of cold defeat.

I was someone, once. Then I was someone else, for a time.
Now I'm just me, doing my own thing. Or so it would seem.

Salami is Hard

I go to the deli at my grocery store
sometimes.
And when I do, there are times
when I order some hard salami.
As soon as they hand me my order,
I say, "*Boy, salami doesn't get
much harder than this!*"
Then I start to stammer.
"*I mean . . . I just,
that didn't come out right.*"
Then I close my eyes, I chuckle.
I bow my head and shyly grab my meat
(you read that correctly).
Then I turn and walk away
feeling a bit lighter on my feet.

Nuts to Soup

A lot of people, like me,
think whales are kind of sacred.
But God, well, he may not hate whales,
but he definitely dislikes them.
Which is likely why he
invented beaches.
I mean, he knows what he's doing.
He's not stupid, you know.
He invented Albert Einstein,
from nuts to soup!
That's right: from nuts to soup.
Would you like me to paint you
a picture?

*Lately, I've been doing The Trout Workout.
It's a lot of swimming. With a little cardio thrown in.*

The Velvet Frog
You can teach a frog how to sing
Dean Martin tunes,
but who will pay
to buy a ticket?
Actually, you know what?
I would.
A chance to see a singing frog?
Are you kidding me?
That's worth the price
of admission!

Integer
I'm pretty sure (68 percent)
that if a frog kissed me
I'd turn into a prince.
I'm just not clear
on the math.

Pabst Blue Ribbon
Back in my dating years,
I used to play old school
sex records while getting ready
for a night out on the town.
Not to get in the mood
or anything like that.
I just dig old school
sex records.

*Sometimes you bare your soul; sometimes
you sell your bear. Life is unpredictable.*

The Constant Gardener
I don't need old school sex records
to get turned on.
I turn myself on.
And if anyone else
happens to get turned on
in the process,
that's just a bonus.

Bedtime Reading
I know this will be viewed
as a radical concept,
but I've always felt that everyone
should get two timeouts
during sex.
The first one, just to pause
and reflect—to strategize.
To study your game plan
in an effort to ensure
that all goals are being met.
And the second one, simply to rest
and catch your breath.
Sex is exhausting!
Although maybe I'm
doing it wrong.
I should really read up
on the topic someday.

I'm at a point in my "comedy" "career" where, if I were eaten by a bear, people would likely say it was for the best. The bear would probably get some kind of commendation.

No Bears in Arkansas

It's easy to lose track of your bearings.
It's also easy to lose track of
your bear.
If you've ever had a bear,
you'll know exactly what I mean.
They're prone to wandering off,
following their muse languidly,
this way or that,
in search of something or other.
Luckily, to find them, you generally
just have to listen for the drone
of angry bees.
Or the sound
of panicked screams.

Revolution in the Head

My head looks a lot
like a minnow bucket.
The shape of it, at least.
Sometimes I wish my head
was a minnow bucket.
If it was, I could sell it
at a yard sale, and probably
get three bucks for it.
Talk about value-added.
That's a 300% profit!!

Someone tried to live vicariously through me once.
That person died of disappointment.

When I'm Bored
Sometimes when I'm bored,
I think about the phone companies
and all the decades they
completely
screwed us over
on long-distance phone calls.
That's always fun.
Good for some laughs.

Prelude to Fusion
I'm always surprised by
how fast a person
can get naked.
Just two moves, and boom!
Full-frontal nudity.
And I'm not talking about
anyone else here, just myself.
I have it down
to a science.

Ladies and gentlemen, you can put a buffalo in a trance, but be sure to stay on your toes. If this little plan of yours goes sideways . . . you're going flying, amigo.

Buffalo Chicken
Whenever I run into someone
who's really buff—be they male
or female—the first thing
I always say is, *"You're so buff!"*
These days, I tend
to walk with
my head down low,
like a buffalo
seeking out a patch
of fresh grass.
I don't want no trouble.
It's just not worth it
anymore.

Barn Muffin (Not a Typo)
I'm a comic and a poet,
not a rancher.
Even so, I've come across
tremendous loads of bullshit
over the course
of my days
here on this earth.
Much like prairie grass,
it just seems to come
with the turf.

*If you really want to understand this world, you have to have a solid
grasp of fluid dynamics. Earth is 70% water. Come on, folks, this isn't
rocket science. Try to keep up, ok?*

Astrophysics
Whenever I meet
an astrophysicist,
I tell them,
"Make up your friggin' mind,
ok?
Do you play for the Astros
or are you a Physicist?"
I meet a lot of
astrophysicists.
It's strange.

Yacht Rock
If I had a boat,
it would rock.
It totally would!
I mean, it's not
rocket science.
It's simple
fluid dynamics.
Read up on it
sometime.
Don't be a jerk.

I hate it when you get to a play late and the usher guides you to your
seats in the dark. Sure, they have that little flashlight. But it's still scary.

Shout-out to Bruce Willis
Out of all *The Vomit Kings*,
die-hard fans usually hope
their drummer will be the one
to actually vomit onstage
on a given night.
People say he doesn't hold
anything back.
They love how he rears back
and lets it all go.
They say he vomits
from the bottom
of his soul.

I'm Confused
As far as your cousin,
the one that I screwed
after the wedding dance
last summer?
I'm a little confused.
You told me to keep an eye
on her and to make sure she
had a good time.
Believe me, she had a good time!
We both did.
I guess I'm not seeing the issue?

*My best pick-up line? "Do you have a paper bag? Because . . . I think
I'm hyper-ventilating." Then, in most cases, I would collapse.*

Chin Music
Suddenly, at the age of 48,
I realized I had an amazing,
beautifully sculpted—as if by
Michelangelo himself—chin.
Not to oversell it, but it's
as though God himself
looked down from Heaven
and said,
"*Let there be chin!*"
And there is!
Or at least
there was.
I guess it depends on
when you're reading this.

Sculpted
My chin is sort of like Medusa.
Only it doesn't turn you
to stone.
On the contrary, seeing it
up close
fills you
with a deep, radiant joy,
a joy you've never known before
and will most likely never know
again,
at least not in this lifetime.
Again, not to oversell it.

*Ladies and gentleman, I don't punch no clock. I'm a pacifist, alright? I
am also unemployed. Just to get that out there.*

Squeeze (Hour Glass)
You can give a clown
a sponge,
but you'll soon wish
you had that sponge back,
to soak up your bitter
tears of regret.
Never give a clown a sponge,
God-dammit.
Never!

Gravity Beats Light Speed
Time does funny
things to all of us.
But in the end,
nobody—
and I mean NOBODY—
is laughing.
I know,
that's grim as hell.
I can't help it.
I'm a comic.

I've never been to Coney Island and I can't sing a lick.
But I love ice cream. Talk about irony.

Like a Glove
I took a roughly 25-year
break from wearing sneakers.
For no one reason.
I simply didn't see a need for them.
They just weren't me, or for me.
That streak was broken when
I became unemployed a while back.
Soon after, I bought a
cheap pair of tennis shoes, and now?
Now I can see the allure.
It's a seductive lifestyle, indeed.
A world of comfort, a world of ease.
It's like living inside of
two dreams.

The Good Old Days
The Romans had
orgies.
We have LinkedIn.
Things were so much better
back then.

If you live next door to me, you're going to see my junk eventually.
That's just the way it is. It's the laws of physics. I can't help you.
No one can. You're doomed.

Gravity Stream
I had a dream about the Apollo 11
mission recently.
In my dream, Neil Armstrong was
Neil Armstrong, and
Michael Collins was Michael Collins.
But Buzz Aldrin
was a Coho salmon.
Only, Neil and Michael were oblivious
to this.
"Don't you get it?!" I wanted to scream.
"All of his jokes about how going to
the moon is a lot like swimming upstream?
He's a fricking Coho salmon in a tiny, little
fish space suit! How are you not seeing this??"
But Neil Armstrong and Michael Collins
could not or simply would not see that
Buzz Aldrin
was a salmon.

Troubled Waters
I'm a word architect.
More than anything,
I like to build bridges with words.
On average, my word bridges
support the weight of a single,
juvenile sardine.
One that hasn't
eaten lunch yet.

I'm not afraid to fish off the company dock. It's so much easier.
A person knows where the fish are. There's no ambiguity.

Fly Away
As a poet, I would compare myself
not to Wadsworth or Longfellow,
but to a really small woodpecker.
One of those birds that
flies into the scene,
pokes around for a bit,
uncovers something
particularly decayed and nasty,
chews on that for a stretch
and then,
without so much as a
"*Hey,*" "*Hello,*" or a "*How do you do?*"
flits off into the distance.

Beat Not Missed
Yeah, I know.
I heard it.
'Really small
woodpecker.'
Way ahead of you.

I know the difference between a salmon and a sponge.
Salmon swim upstream.

Three Hour Cruise
This world has swallowed me whole,
and on more than one occasion.
What's left of me
is that which made it through, fell out
the other side and splashed down
into the sea.
I'll let you draw your own conclusions
as to what the exact composition
of that end product
might be.

Box Office
I'm a huge f-----g fan of
the em dash.
Huge fan!
I simply cannot get
enough—of them.
They add so much
to any given sentence.
Look at the movie
There Will Be Blood.
Now, with a title like that,
I could pretty much
take it or leave it.
But toss in an em dash . . .
There Will Be Blood—Or Will There?
Well, now I have to know!

I think comedy should be regulated—like a utility.

The Ruins

I always send my new material
to this archaeologist friend of mine.
She digs it.
That's her job: to dig up stuff and
figure out what it was and what it meant
to the people that made it or once
possessed it.
My friend is really good
at what she does.
And she loves pottery.
Loves, loves, loves it!
But she cannot stand poetry.
Especially my poetry.
I really don't know why I use her
as a sounding board.
There's a part of me that suspects
I might secretly be a masochist.
If that were true, then at least
some of this
would make sense.

I always like it when someone says to me, "I'm not going to fight you."
That tells me, "This is a fight I can win!"

Customer Service
I hate when you walk into Costco
and someone
punches you right in the face
and says,
"Welcome to Costco, asshole!"
If it wasn't for their truly excellent prices,
I would likely
do my shopping
elsewhere.

Jeff Edamame
One of my roughly 38 fans (give or take)
approached me recently
and said, "I know you often
make up names and people
in your work, but I have to know—I must!
Is Jeff Edamame real?"
I smiled broadly and said,
"Is Jeff Edamame real? Why,
of course he's real! He couldn't be
more real if he tried!"
They seemed relieved by this
and continued cheerfully on their way.
Meanwhile, I patted the small protrusion
in my shirt pocket and whispered,
"Did you hear that, old buddy?"
A few moments later, I chuckled and said,
"I know! That's what I told them!"

I stopped by The Reluctant Trout recently. The food was fine, but they
really need to shit or get off the pot. I know I'm right about this.

Ben Franklin's Kite
When I read my old poems,
I get a jolt.
I taste real lightning.
That guy, I think, that younger me,
he could very well
change the world someday.
Today's me, the me that I see
in the mirror each and every day,
he ain't gonna change shit.
He's just going to sit around
all day and eat day-old bread and
string cheese.
Pardon my French.
Por favor—if you
please.

Raindrops Keep Falling
If you wear pants
in the rain,
they're going to
get wet.
There's an easy solution
to this conundrum.
Do not overthink it.

*I don't much care about the past. I'm only mildly
interested in the present. And the future? Meh.*

Backing Track
I never set out
to change the recording industry,
which is fortunate.
Because as far as I can tell,
I've had no impact
on the recording industry
whatsoever.

My Way
If it were all to end
tomorrow,
you know,
what would there be to say?
I've squeezed my share
of lemons.
I've diced my share
of limes.
I really
can't complain.

Ladies and gentlemen, I'm in one hell of a bind.
I'm too beautiful to live . . . and too sexy to die.

Another Friend of Mine
I jumped out of an airplane once.
Wearing a parachute, obvi.
So did my friend Steve*.
But he liked it so much that he
went out and got certified
and then went on to do dozens more
solo jumps.
Which was great, really.
Just terrific.
We get it, Steve!
You're not afraid of death, are you, Steve?
You're so much better than
all the rest of us, aren't you, Steve?
It's too bad everyone isn't more like you
—isn't it, Steve?
The world would be such a
better place,
wouldn't it?!

It, ah, it actually would
be a much better place.
I know I don't say this
nearly enough, Steve**
but I admire you.
You're very brave.

*Just for a little additional background, Steve is my imaginary friend.

**Fun fact: I actually have two imaginary friends named Steve. Even I
sometimes have trouble keeping them straight.

Egret Window
I have this friend
—maybe we all do—
who always gets everything
just a little bit wrong.
Her three favorite actors?
Diesel Washington,
Daryl Streep and
and Mark Buffalo.
Her favorite Renaissance painter?
Boughtacello.

Lobster Clatter
This is not easy to write about.
Oh, who am I kidding?
It's remarkably easy to write about.
I am, very much,
like a lobster in bed.
It can be more than a little overwhelming,
by just about any measure.
All the pinching, clawing,
clutching, clacking.
Sometimes I can't watch.

All the Pretty Horses
You can lead
a horse to water.
Really, anyone can.
It isn't rocket science.

No one knows what it's like to have sex with a salmon.
Not even a salmon.

Appetizer Splatter
It's important to have
dreams, even if they
blow up
in your face.
That way, at least,
you'll know how they taste.

More Dessert
Recently, as a joke,
I led a horse into a small-town bar
owned by a good friend of mine.
When the bartender noticed us,
he frowned and said,
"*The nearest source of fresh water
is at least fifteen miles from here.*"
I looked at the horse and bowed my head
sadly, in defeat.
"*I can't even do this much right,*" I murmured,
as we turned around and clip-clopped slowly
towards the exit.

*We've all said some things. Who knows what
any of them meant? Not me. I wasn't listening.*

Picking and a-Grinning

When I was younger,
I hated the sound of my voice.
It was so damn thin, nasally.
Then I read a book which said
if you're projecting properly,
you should feel
the bridge of your nose vibrate
when you speak.
However, to feel that vibration,
you have to place a finger
along your nose while you're talking.
So if you passed me in another car
back then, as I was driving down
the road, probably heading east,
now you know
that I wasn't picking my nose
while talking to myself.
Not every single time,
at least.

When my dog wears a neck scarf, everyone thinks it's the cutest thing ever. When I wear a neck scarf, everyone thinks I'm an a-hole. Life isn't fair.

Correct Me If I'm Wrong
People say to me, *"Dan, it's the 20th-Century.*
Why are you still mucking about
with poetry? What's your deal?"
I generally reply, *"My deal?*
What's my deal?
I'm trying to heal this
broken wheel, amigo. That's my deal.
What's your deal?
Hm? Hm??"
Hmm.
Then I stand up straight tall and say,
"So it sounds to me like one of us
is a goddam folk hero, and one of us
doesn't have much to say at all.
That's what it's sounding like to me."

Jade in Amber
My whole life, I've viewed things
through this ironic prism.
And for a long time, I kind of
resented that—being walled up,
cut off.
Isolated
from the rest
of the world.
Now I'm not so sure.
I kind of like it
in here.

Ladies and gentlemen, I'm a poet who can hit the open jump shot.
There are only four of us in the whole world. Two of us are in Spain.
One of us is in Helsinki.

If You Ever
If you ever meet someone
who knows what they're doing,
grab hold of them.
Seize hold of them
tightly,
around both ankles,
and never, ever let them go.
I mean, ever.
And if they tell you
that they have to leave,
beg them to take you with them.
There's no shame in it.
Nothing that you can't live with.

U-S-A!
We're almost at the end.
This is the part of the book
where I know I'm supposed
to 'finish strong.'
But I don't want to finish strong.
I want to finish weak
and complain about it
every single step
of the way.
That's always the route to take.
That's what made
this country great.

It's a good thing I don't have any pride. Otherwise,
all of this would be pretty darn embarrassing.

One for the Hecklers
I hope there's a crosswalk
somewhere
in the quiet streets
of your mind
for all your
pedestrian thoughts.

Happy Hour
Awhile back,
I was just sitting around
when I injured my hand badly
trying to break a table in half
with a sweet karate chop.
And, man, did that hurt.
It hurt a whole bunch!
So I stepped back and
kicked a barstool
really, really hard.
Then the bartender barked,
"Are you going to order something?!"
What's the matter with this place?
Doesn't anyone have a heart??

Just because my wife wears the pants in our family,
that doesn't mean the rest of us are weirdos.

Religious Awakening
I'm not going to say
much more about
screwing your cousin—
after that wedding dance
last summer.
But if I might, could I just
add this?
It was like sliding into butter
hand-churned by God herself.
It was life-changing,
I mean that.
And that's the last time I'll ever
bring it up.
There's no need to dwell on it
any further.
I'm pretty sure you know
what I'm saying.

Sometimes when I give myself a sponge bath,
I find myself feeling bad for the sponge.

Free Association
Do you remember that time
you came on the radio?
I'm sure it was very exciting for you
and for all the people that
know you.
Everyone admires the reflection
of fame, no matter how large
or how small.
Meanwhile, as I sat there listening,
listening almost as though
I was in a storeroom trance,
all I could think was,
*"This is the prick
that screwed my cousin
last summer
—after that wedding dance!"*

*You've been very kind, Ladies and Gentlemen, very kind, indeed. But
I can't do this alone. How about a big round of applause for that ripe,
red tomato above us? Without her, we'd all be encased in thick sheets of
ice. Let's give it up, okay?*

Comedy Album was (kind of*) recorded before a live studio audience

June 17, 2019—at Sisyphus Brewing in Minneapolis, Minnesota USA

*In a way.

Tour's over. Home soon. Will hope to find my glasses.
—H.

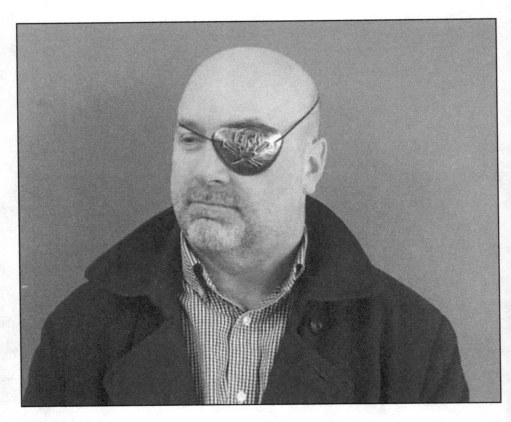

Often referred to as 'The Dramamine Pirate,' Dan Hendrickson is a comic, screenwriter and poet, who lives in Minneapolis. Comedy Album is the modestly-awaited follow-up effort to 2017's *Dark Glasses*. Prior to that, Hendrickson authored and self-published a handful of works comprised mostly of experimental poetry and slapdash philosophy, under the pseudonym Henry Rifle. He describes those off-the-cuff, under the radar efforts (*Shooting Gallery, Bullet Train, A Bullet West* and *Ballistics Report*) as 'poetry for people who can't stand poetry.'

Whereas those early collections were largely comprised of casual bon mots and barbed bonbons, *Dark Glasses* was a balanced meal; a comedic examination of politics, absurdity, current events and personal identity. As for this effort (*Comedy Album*), it's a blast of pure seltzer; an old-fashioned kick in the seat of the pants.

"What I wanted to do was make a comedy album, like my heroes, Bob Newhart and Richard Pryor," Hendrickson says. "But what I didn't want to do was have to rent a microphone and a speaker. Technology depresses me—and I'm sure as hell not made out of money."

Hendrickson's musings, video clips, long-winded digressions and more still can be found at *dan-hendrickson.com*.

CPSIA information can be obtained
at www.ICGtesting.com
Printed in the USA
LVHW090844051020
667943LV00002B/123

9 781938 237317